BUILD AN EMPIRE

Implement your business ideas as an entrepreneur

Joy Gabriel M.

Copyright © 2022 by Joy Gabriel M.

All rights reserved.

Before this document is duplicated or reproduced in any manner, the publisher's consent must be gained. Therefore, the contents within can neither be stored electronically, transferred, nor kept in a database. Neither in part nor full can the document be copied, scanned, faxed, or retained without approval from the publisher or creator.

Table Of Contents

Introduction   4

Startup Business Ideas   5

Finances and Capital   9

Branding   16

Connection with Customers   22

The Right Marketing Strategy   28

Analyze Your Business Legal Structure   35

Researching The Dream And Lease   48

Trust   55

Development   59

Testing Your Business Ideas   61

Introduction

You need to ensure you plan completely prior to beginning a business, yet understand that things will without a doubt turn out badly. To maintain an effective business, you should adjust to evolving circumstances.

Leading inside and out statistical surveying on your field and the socioeconomics of your potential client is a significant piece of making a marketable strategy. This includes running reviews, holding center gatherings, and exploring Web optimization and public information.

Before you begin selling your item or administration, you really want to develop your image and get a following of individuals who are prepared to bounce when you open your entryways for business.

This book is for business people who need to become familiar with the nuts and bolts of steps of beginning another business.

Errands like naming the business and making a logo are self-evident, however, what might be said about the significant stages? Whether it's deciding your business structure or making a point-by-point promoting system, the responsibility can rapidly stack up. As opposed to wasting your time and speculating about where to begin, follow these tips to change your business from a light over your head to a domain.

Startup Business Ideas

In case you're pondering starting a business, you likely at this point have considered what you want to sell on the web, on the other hand, if nothing else the market you want to enter. Do a quick journey for existing associations in your picked industry. Find out what current brand pioneers are doing and strategize how you can get to the next level. If you figure your business can convey something else associations don't, or you have areas of strength and are ready to make a field-tried technique.

Put forth objectives

Persistently start with why

It is perfect to know why you are shipping off your business. In this cycle, it may be shrewd to isolate whether the business serves a singular goal or a business place objective. Exactly when your goal is revolved around tending to a need in the business community, the degree of your business will continually be greater than a business that is expected to serve a singular need.

Consider differentiating

Another decision is to open a foundation of a spread-out association. The thought, brand following, and game plan are at this point set up; all you need is a fair region and the vital assets to sponsor your action.

Conceptualize your business name

Despite which decision you pick, understanding the reasoning behind your thought is fundamental. Scarcely any cautions go to financial specialists against creating a system or conceptualizing a business name before making sure about the idea's worth.

Make sense of your objective clients

Over and over, people skip shipping off their business without effective money management energy to examine who their clients will be and why they would have to buy from them or enroll them.

You need to make sense of why you want to work with these clients: do you have an excitement about simplifying people's lives? Then again, appreciate making workmanship to convey tone to their existence? Perceiving these reactions makes sense of your principal objective. Third, you want to describe how you will offer this advantage to your clients and how to convey that value to such an extent that they will pay.

During the ideation stage, you need to sort out the huge nuances. In case the idea isn't something you're lively about then again if there's not a business opportunity for your creation, it might be an optimal chance to conceptualize various considerations.

Make an attractive technique

When you have your idea set up, you need to present yourself with several huge requests: What is the inspiration driving your business? Who are you presenting to? What are your definitive goals? How should you support your startup costs? These requests can be answered in a richly created field-tried technique.

A lot of blunders are made by new associations hustling into things disregarding these pieces of the business. You need to search your objective client base. Who will buy your thing or organization? In case you can't find verification that there's an interest in your idea, why trouble?

Lead factual studying

Factual reviewing helps you with sorting out your objective client, their necessities, tendencies, and direct as well as your industry and opponents. Various privately owned business specialists propose gathering fragment information and guiding a serious assessment to more promptly handle significant entryways and cutoff points inside your market.

The best free organizations have things or organizations that are isolated from the resistance. This influences your serious scene and grants you to give novel worth to anticipated clients.

A marketable strategy assists you with sorting out where your organization is going, how it will defeat any likely troubles, and what you really want to support it. At the point when you're prepared to put pen to paper, these formats can help.

Finances and Capital

Whether you choose a bank credit, a private supporter, an administration award, or a business incubator, every one of these wellsprings of funding enjoys explicit benefits and hindrances as well as standards they will use to assess your business.

Here is an outline of wellsprings of funding for new companies:

Individual speculation

While beginning a business, your most memorable financial backer ought to act naturally: either with your own money or with security on your resources. This demonstrates to financial backers and investors that you have a drawn-out obligation to your task and that you are prepared to face challenges.

Love cash

This is cash credited by a companion, guardians, family, or companions. Financial backers and brokers think about this as "patient capital", which is cash that will be reimbursed later as your business benefits increment.

While getting love cash, you ought to know that:

Loved ones don't often have a lot of capital
They might need to have value in your business
A business relationship with family or companions ought to never be messed with

Funding

The main thing to remember is that funding isn't really for all business visionaries. Right all along, you ought to know that financial speculators are searching for innovation-driven organizations and organizations with high-development potential in areas like data innovation, communication, and biotechnology.

Financial speculators take a valuable position in the organization to assist it with completing a promising however higher risk project. This includes surrendering a possession or value in your business to an outside party. Financial speculators likewise expect a solid profit from their venture, frequently produced when the business begins offering offers to the general population. Make certain to search for financial backers who carry important experience and information to your business.

BDC has a funding group that supports driving edge organizations decisively situated in a promising business sector. Like most other funding organizations, it engages in new businesses with high-development potential, liking to zero in on significant mediations when an organization needs a lot of support to get laid out in its market.

Angels

Angels are by and large affluent people or resigned organization leaders who put straightforwardly in little firms possessed by others. They are much of the time chiefs in their field who not just contribute their experience and organization of contacts yet additionally their specialized or potentially the executive's information. Angels will generally fund the beginning phases of the business with interests in the request for $25,000 to $100,000. Institutional financial speculators benefit bigger ventures, in the request for $1,000,000.

In return for taking a chance with their cash, they claim all authority to direct the organization's administration rehearses. In substantial terms, this frequently includes a seat on the directorate and a confirmation of straightforwardness.

Angels will generally stay under the radar. To meet them, you need to contact specific affiliations or search sites on angels. The National Angel Capital Organization (NACO) is an umbrella association that helps construct limits concerning Canadian private supporters. You can look at their part's catalog for thoughts regarding who to contact in your district.

Business incubators

Business incubators (or accelerators) for the most part center around the super advanced area by offering help for new organizations in different progressive phases. Be that as it may, there are likewise neighborhood financial improvement incubators, which are centered around regions like work creation, renewal, and facilitating and sharing administrations.

Ordinarily, incubators will welcome future organizations and other young organizations to share their premises, as well as their regulatory, strategic, and specialized assets. For instance, an incubator could share the utilization of its research centers with the goal that another business can create and test its items all the more economically before starting its creation.

By and large, the incubating stage can endure as long as two years. When the item is prepared, the business ordinarily passes on the incubator's premises to enter its modern creation stage and is all alone.

Organizations that get this sort of help frequently work inside cutting-edge areas like biotechnology, data innovation, media, or modern innovation.

Government awards and endowments

Government offices give support, for example, awards and appropriations that might be accessible to your business. The site of the Public authority of Canada gives a complete posting of different taxpayer-supported initiatives at the government and commonplace levels.

Rules

Getting awards can be intense. There might be areas of strength and the standards for grants are frequently rigid. By and large, most awards expect you to match the assets you are being given and this sum fluctuates extraordinarily, contingent upon the granter. For instance, an examination award might expect you to see just 40% of the complete expense.

For the most part, you should give:

A point-by-point project portrayal
A clarification of the advantages of your undertaking
A point-by-point work plan with full expenses
Subtleties of significant experience and foundation on key supervisors
Finished application structures when proper

Most analysts will survey your proposition in light of the following rules:

Importance
Approach
Advancement
Evaluation of ability
Need for the award

A portion of the pain points where competitors neglect to get awards to include:

The exploration/work isn't significant
Ineligible geographic area
Candidates neglect to convey the significance of their thoughts
The proposition doesn't give areas of strength
The examination plan is unfocused
There is a ridiculous measure of work
Reserves are not coordinated

Bank advances

Bank advances are the most usually involved wellspring of subsidizing for little and medium-sized organizations. Consider the way that all banks offer various benefits, whether it's customized administration or modified reimbursement. It's really smart to look around and track down the bank that meets your particular requirements.

As a general rule, you ought to realize financiers are searching for organizations with sound history and that have great credit. Smart isn't sufficient; it must be upheld with a strong strategy. Fire-up credits will likewise ordinarily require individual assurance from the business visionaries.

BDC offers to fire up support to business visionaries at the beginning of a stage or initial year of deals. You may likewise have the option to defer the chief installments for as long as a year.

Branding

Branding is the most common way of making areas of strength for a view of an organization, its items, or administrations in the client's brain by consolidating such components as logo, plan, statement of purpose, and a predictable subject all through showcasing correspondences. Successful branding assists organizations with separating themselves from their rivals and constructing a reliable client base. Ensure you make a steady brand with the goal that your clients take delight in your omnichannel presence.

Branding in-store can be different from web-based branding, you need to stress over situating items and props that can impact how a client encounters your image. Branding in-store is more experiential as individuals can stroll around and get things, though clients online are encountering a two-layered scene. Certain components of branding are predictable both on the web and available. These incorporate predictable symbolism and logos.

Why is branding significant?

An extraordinary brand can tremendously affect your main concern by giving you an upper hand over your opponents and aiding you to procure and hold clients at a much lower cost. In online business, where new organizations (and hence, new contenders) are jumping up each day, a laid-out brand can be an important resource in bringing clients and producing benefits.

Whether or not you're putting time and exertion into making a convincing brand or giving no consideration to it at all, your business has a brand. Notwithstanding, it very well might be unique to how you expected to be seen.

Via cautiously developing your image through stories, relationships, showcasing messages, and visual resources, you have the chance of forming your clients' assumptions and making a remarkable bond that goes past the buying-selling relationship.

Great branding is vital while promoting is strategic. At the point when you lay out the higher targets and characterize your image guarantee, you can begin creating a showcasing plan that is equipped for accomplishing those objectives.

Branding is a perplexing interaction that requires cautious preparation and a determined approach. In a perfect world, you ought to have your branding procedure worked out before sending off to try not to work in reverse to attempt adjusting your store to client assumptions. A solid brand is not difficult to connect with and draws on values that reverberate well with the interest group.

Figure out your clients

To convey successfully, you need to distinguish the components that impact your objective clients and spotlight on utilizing them. What do they like? What persuades and draws them? What do they like about your image?

Characterize your image persona

A brand persona is the character of your business wherein you will convey client encounters. It will be unequivocally impacted by the bits of knowledge you figure out how to accumulate about your objective clients. What manner of speaking will suit them? What kind of language will make the best difference? What pictures will stand out for them?

Crystalize your image guarantee

What is a definitive commitment you're making to your clients? How might your items/administrations improve their life? How are you going to convey this commitment? 66% of purchasers think straightforwardness is one of a brand's most appealing characteristics.

Wonderful your visual resources

Online customers don't have the advantage of touching and feeling the items they purchase, so the visual experience is essential. A brand's visual resources are the forward-looking components, for example, the web composition, textual styles and typography, variety range, logo and promotion plans as well as the bundling and unpacking experience you make. It's a strong marking instrument that arrives at its pinnacle when every one of the different moving parts is predictable and works agreeably. Research shows that having a significant mark variety will expand the opportunity for clients to perceive your image by 80%.

Refine client experience

Even though you have little command over how your clients will eventually feel about your image, you ought to put forth a valiant effort to ensure each collaboration and contact point you have with your clients is lined up with your image guarantee and observes your image rules.
70% of purchasers say that the main thing brands can do to further develop their experience is "knowing them". This will incorporate everything from your merchandise exchanges to transportation, courses of action to email advertising, communications and that's only the tip of the iceberg.

You can work on your publicizing

Your business will not have the option to get much of anywhere without publicizing. Branding and publicizing remain forever inseparable. If you have any desire to have better publicizing for your business, you will have to chip away at making a brand first.
While you're publicizing your business, you maintain that everything should be durable and address your business'

personality and values. This can be difficult when you haven't set aside some margin to frame your image. On the off chance that you're publicizing without strong branding, you're passing up a ton of extraordinary chances to make a successful mission. Integrating branding into your publicizing will assist with expanding acknowledgment of your image when it's all integrated.

Make sure to offer in return

Something as straightforward as saying thank you to your dependable clients can go quite far in reinforcing your image picture. Show appreciation by running extraordinary projects or advancements, offering intermittent unconditional gifts, or broadening limits. It's a dependable method for building long-haul associations with your clients and refining your image.

A business branding is surprisingly significant. Outwardly, your image might seem like it comprises just components like logos and varieties, however, your image is the whole personality of your business. Your image gives you character.

Branding has forever been an indispensable piece of business, however, it very well might be more significant now than any other time in recent memory. With web-based entertainment, purchasers get presented with new brands consistently. This can be perfect for purchasers who have a lot of choices and can do research to view the best one, however it makes it harder for organizations.

Connection With Customers

It takes something other than giving quality items and administration to have an effective business, your standing can be made or broken by your client support.

In the age of the Web, it is simpler than any time in recent memory to say some unacceptable thing, and the outcomes can be substantially more harmful than in days past. Quite a long while prior, on the off chance that a supervisor or President said some unacceptable thing in a magazine or paper, it adversely affected their profile, however, presently fresh insight about a significant violation of social norms can spread across the web surprisingly fast.

In like manner, mistreating clients can draw in regrettable consideration and can pursue potential clients away, maybe into the arms of your rivals. While cash can purchase you smooth introductions, the best online courses, and superstar supports, no measure of subsidizing can get you the regard of a solid client base.

How might you reinforce the connection between your business and your clients?

Treat your Clients as Individuals, not simply Cash Distributors

Organizations can without much of a stretch tragically underestimate clients; enormous partnerships and little firms the same can start to see their clients as cash distributors as opposed to individuals.

This is a tremendous issue in the long haul. Center around regarding individuals as you might want to be dealt with: focus on their remarks across web-based entertainments, direct overviews, and give a lot of contact choices: live visits, telephone numbers, email locations, and accommodation structures ought to be in every way promptly open.

Embrace the Speed, Straightforwardness, and Viability of Web-based Entertainment

Web-based entertainment has fundamentally had an impact on the way the vast majority of us convey. Though messaging supplanted the call, web-based entertainment has supplanted the text. Communicating something specific through Facebook or Twitter is speedy, straightforward, and permits you to connect extra media with less quarrel than while sending messages.

You ought to as of now be utilizing web-based entertainment to speak with clients, however, try not to extend yourself excessively far across them all: track down the organizations with the best centralization of clients and spotlight on them. While you might need to keep up with profiles on a wide assortment of organizations, don't simply have similar posts across them all; tailor your presents to the greatest dynamic segment.

Energize your client assistance administrators to hold back nothing

The more drawn-out clients (existing or potential) need to hang tight for replies to questions or complaints, the more outlandish they are to trust you. You ought to likewise ensure you're answering criticism: tune in via web-based entertainment however much you talk, while possibly not all the more so.

Make Communications as Straightforward as could be expected

You want to converse with your clients where they are and today they invest quite a bit of their energy utilizing social and versatile applications and scrutinizing sites. It's sort of odd to anticipate that these clients should get a different telephone and start from the very beginning again when they need to converse with you.

The numbers show that your clients are spending increasingly more of their Web time on cell phone, so you want serious areas of strength for an application methodology. Fortunately, there are tool compartments accessible that permit you to install voice and video squarely into your versatile applications as well. What's more, organizations can likewise offer types of assistance in the cloud to help you consistently associate with versatile clients overall while keeping up with excellent calls.

Make Trustworthiness Your Arrangement

The web has given purchasers to a greater extent a voice and made them significantly more business insights. On the off chance that an organization is lying or attempting to con them, they will ensure others learn about it across web-based entertainment, web journals, and different outlets.

Building more grounded security with your clients comes down to trust: on the off chance that your objective segment feels they have practically zero motivation to trust you, for what reason would it be a good idea for them to keep on giving their cash to you rather than to your rival?

While speaking with clients (utilizing web-based entertainment, email, or telephone), show sympathy towards their particular requirements and conditions. Keep up with your trustworthiness by conveying items, administrations, or reactions when you say you will and spotlight on having a decent effect on clients as opposed to pursuing the following dollar.

Center around inbound showcasing as opposed to outbound

Outbound showcasing is, basically, based around interfering (or in any event, barging in on) your clients' days: whether this is through television promotions, non-mentioned advertising messages, unapproved instant messages, or pop-ups on irrelevant sites, such strategies appear to bother more than allure.

On the off chance that an individual from people, in general, gets such countless meddlesome promotions from an organization, they will be given a negative impression, and subsequently, they will be exceptionally improbable to search out your business at any point in the near future.

Inbound advertising (otherwise called "pull showcasing", instead of the norm "push"- based rehearses utilized by certain organizations) can be considerably more fulfilling and assemble entrust with your clients.

How might you attempt this for your business?

Make important substance to take care of clients' concerns: blog entries, downloadable digital books, recordings, webcasts, and more can all offer supportive data, (for example, giving experiences into creation processes, help with a specific piece of programming, or whatever else pertinent to your business).

Assuming this material is adequate, clients may likewise impart it to other people, driving more traffic in your direction and possibly helping change rates.

Building more grounded bonds with your clients is essential to guarantee life span and dependability, so contribute time, exertion, and assets to finding what they need. The more you can tailor your administrations as well as items to your objective segment, the greater the extent of return you are probably going to get.

The Right Marketing Strategy

Advertisement

Advertising can drive achievement, in both the long haul and the present moment. Make an adaptable and executable promoting procedure to boost your profit from speculation. Ponder what is one of a kind about your business and how to capitalize on it and consider the most effective way to arrive at the clients who require your item or administration. Consider what your rivals are doing and see what you can improve to give you a benefit over them. Entrepreneurs ought to research business subjects for showcasing tips on the most proficient method to advance their business. Put all of this into a Showcasing plan, and set that strategy in motion. Return to and survey the arrangement consistently to adjust to changing economic situations and incorporate new special exercises or those you have made to progress.

Take a look at your promoting technique

The right showcasing system and execution is crucial to making progress of your business, so constructing a very much viewed as however adaptable promoting plan, which you can survey and repeat consistently, ought to be the main concern. A few special exercises should be possible for nothing, yet all in all, you will require some speculation, so put away however much you can for those areas that are probably going to drive the best profit from the venture. Not certain where to begin? Come with me.

Get on top of your funds

Numerous business people find it a test, it's essential to progress. This implies setting monetary targets, following your income, and being prepared to source reserves when you want them. Our monetary goals will assist you with getting set.

Put resources into your group

It's never an error to put resources into spurring and connecting with your workers. Everyone works better when they feel esteemed and compensated, in addition to a cheerful group around you, you'll find it more straightforward to draw in new staff and keep hold of the ones you have. Remunerating workers doesn't have to cost the earth.

Contrast plans with real deals

Thoroughly consider what turned out diversely and what didn't, and why. Before long, you'll contemplate your advertising methodology, target markets, promoting messages, clients, channels, bundling, conveyance, grumblings, and contenders. I'm astounded at the amount of business, and the business arranging process turns around the contrast between arranged and real deals.

What's more, presently you're arranging.

Converse with all-around picked individuals

Interesting how long it goes by for most entrepreneurs without truly talking even to your clients, considerably less to a couple of individuals who aren't your clients yet could be. I was stunned whenever I first got it done. I felt like I conversed with clients frequently, yet that isn't anything to what you get when you commit time and have a genuine discussion.

First, make a decent rundown

At any rate, try not to swindle yourself and talk just to individuals you generally converse with. Stretch yourself further and discover certain individuals you don't have any idea about, so you get a new look. Ask them for their time, not as an overview taker but rather as the proprietor or supervisor of the business. Many individuals will turn you down, yet on the off chance that the discussion is outlined right, you'll discover certain individuals intrigued.

Begin the discussion with intriguing inquiries. The primary two or three inquiries are basic to the progress of the discussion. Get their advantage. Wake their interest.

Also, presently you're arranging.

Envision your optimal client. Give her an orientation, occupation, family (or not), kids (or not), course to work, most loved magazines, network shows, side interests, sites, music, and films. If she possesses a vehicle, what brand, what model? Envision the most loved excursions.

Presently envision how she tracks down your business. What does he like about you, and what does she despise? What prompts him to search for you? Where does she look? What does he educate others regarding your business?

How would you like to be portrayed by your clients to their companions? What is it that you need to make them separate you, from them?

Ponder that, envision that, and presently you're arranging.

Envision a superior future

Where your business may be a long time from now on the off chance that things go all around well. What will your office or store or plant seem to be a long time from now? What will you be selling? How different is it based on the thing you're selling today? Who will you be selling as well? How different will that be from who you offer to the present time?

Some would call this dreaming. Be that as it may, dreaming ahead, dreaming what's in store, is a crucial piece of business arranging. Dream it, then center it, and set the moves toward getting it going. Then track and follow up, and make due.

Comprehend the Responsibility and Difficulties Engaged with Beginning a Business

Beginning a business is an enormous responsibility. Business people frequently neglect to see the value in the huge measure of time, assets, and energy expected to begin and grow a business.

Here are probably the greatest difficulties in the beginning and growing a business:

Concocting an extraordinary and remarkable item or administration
Having major areas of strength for and vision for the business
Having adequate capital and income
Tracking down incredible workers
Terminating terrible workers rapidly in a manner that doesn't bring about lawful risk
Working more than you anticipated
Not getting deterred by dismissals from clients
Dealing with your time productively
Keeping a sensible work/life balance
Knowing when to turn your procedure

Keeping up with the endurance to continue to go in any event, when it's extreme

Direct people to Your Site

While whole books have been composed on this subject, the vital ways of directing people to your site are as per the following:

Fabricate an extraordinary site with loads of superior grade, a unique substance that is web index upgraded.
Has brilliant web-based entertainment intended to drive traffic from Facebook, Twitter, LinkedIn, and other free virtual entertainment destinations?
Get connections to your site from excellent destinations.

Ensure Somebody Hasn't Previously Imagined Your Incredible Groundbreaking Thought

Here are the vital activities on the off chance that you have an incredible new creation thought:

Do a Google search on the watchwords related to your development.
Do an inquiry online of the U.S. Patent and Trademark Office
If nothing comes up and you need to get a patent for your thought, employ a patent legal counselor.

Try not to Overdo it on a Strategy

It's valuable to concoct a strategy to thoroughly consider how you need to help the improvement of the item or administration, promotion, or monetary projections, and that's only the tip of the iceberg. Furthermore, you ought to then get input from confided-in business and money counselors. Be that as it may, don't overdo it with a 50-page field-tested strategy. Truly, numerous new companies need to veer off from their arrangement as the business creates.

Analyze Your Legal Structure

Enlist an Accomplished Startup Lawyer

You want a shrewd business legal counselor for your organization, one who has routinely shaped and prompted numerous different business visionaries and who has some expertise in new companies. An accomplished startup attorney can help you:

Consolidate

Draw up agreements with any prime supporters

Plan key arrangements for the business

Set up an investment opportunity plan for representatives

Guide you through potential HR landmines

Get ready defensive proposition letters to imminent workers

Assist you with arranging terms with planned financial backers

Limit your expected lawful liabilities

Safeguard your thoughts and innovations (through copyrights, licenses, and non-exposure arrangements)

In an off-track work to save money on costs, new companies frequently enlist unpracticed legitimate direction. Instead of expenditure the cash important to employ equipped legitimate direction, pioneers will frequently enlist attorneys who are companions, family members, or other people who offer enormous expense limits. In doing as such, the pioneers deny themselves the guidance of experienced legitimate direction who might assist them with staying away from numerous serious lawful issues.

Get suggestions for legal advisors from different business people and financial speculators. Ensure you have decent compatibility with the lawyer. Meet with a few possible lawyers before you pursue the last choice.

Enrolling your organization

Before you can enroll your organization, you really want to conclude what sort of substance it is. Your business structure lawfully influences everything from how you record your charges to your own responsibility in the event that something turns out badly.

Sole Ownership

In the event that you own the business completely without anyone else and want to be liable for all obligations and commitments, you can enlist for sole ownership. Be informed that this course can influence your own credit.

Partnership

On the other hand, a business association, as its name infers, implies that at least two individuals are held and by at risk as entrepreneurs. You don't need to do it single-handedly in the event that you can find a colleague with corresponding abilities to your own. It's typically really smart to add somebody in with the general mish-mash to assist your business with thriving.

If you have any desire to isolate your own responsibility from your organization's obligation, you might need to consider shaping one of a few sorts of companies. Although each kind of partnership is dependent upon various rules, this lawful design by and large makes a business a different element from its proprietors, and, subsequently, companies can claim property, expect responsibility, settle charges, enter agreements, sue, and be sued like some other person. Partnerships are appropriate for new organizations that plan on opening up to the world or looking for financing from investors soon.

Restricted obligation organization

One of the most widely recognized structures for independent ventures is the Limited Liability Company (LLC). This mixture structure has the legitimate securities of an enterprise while considering the tax breaks of an organization.

At last, it depends on you to figure out which sort of substance is best for your ongoing requirements and future business objectives. It's essential to find out about the different legitimate business structures accessible. On the off chance that you're battling to decide, it's anything but an impractical notion to examine the choice with a business or lawful counselor.

Register with the public authority and IRS

You should acquire an assortment of permits to function before you can legitimately work your business. For example, you want to enlist your business with bureaucratic, state, and nearby legislatures. There are a few records you should draw out before enlisting.

Articles of fuse and working arrangements

To turn into a formally approved business element, you should enroll with the public authority. Businesses need an articles of fuse report, which incorporates your business name, business reason, corporate design, stock subtleties, and other data about your organization. Also, some LLCs should provide a working understanding.

Carrying on with work as (DBA)

In the event that you don't have articles of joining or a working understanding, you should enroll your business name, which can be your lawful name, a made-up DBA name (assuming that you are the sole owner), or the name you've concocted for your organization. You may likewise need to do whatever it takes to reserve your business name for extra lawful insurance.

Most states expect you to get a DBA. In the event that you're in an overall association or ownership working under an imaginary name, you might have to apply for a DBA declaration. It's ideal to contact or visit your neighborhood province agent's office and get some information about unambiguous prerequisites and charges. By and large, there is an enrollment expense included.

Employer Identification Number (EIN)

After registering your business, you must get a business recognizable proof number from the IRS. While this isn't needed for sole ownerships without any representatives, you might need to apply for one, at any rate, to keep your own and business charges isolated, or essentially to save yourself the difficulty later in the event that you choose to recruit somebody. The IRS has given an organized plan to decide if you will require an EIN to maintain your business. In the event that you in all actuality do require an EIN, you can enlist online for nothing.

Annual tax documents

You likewise need to document specific structures to satisfy your government and state annual duty commitments. The structures you are not set in stone by your business structure. You should thoroughly take a glance at your state's site for data on state-explicit and neighborhood charge commitments.

Businesses and self-employed entities in specific exchanges are expected to convey proficient licenses. An illustration of an expert permit to operate is a commercial driver's license (CDL). People with a CDL are permitted to work on specific sorts of vehicles, for example, transports, tank trucks, and semi-trucks. A CDL is separated into three (3) classes: Class A, Class B, and Class C.

You ought to likewise check with your city and state to see whether you really want a vendor's grant that approves your business to gather deals charge from your clients. A dealer's grant goes by various names, including resale license, exchange license, license permit, affiliate grant, resale ID, state charge ID number, affiliate number, affiliate permit grant, or testament of power.

It's critical to take note that these prerequisites and names differ from one state to another. You can enroll for a dealer's grant through the state government site of the state (s) you're carrying on with work in.

Consider the Means You Ought to Take to Safeguard Your Protected innovation

It is vital to safeguard your organization's intellectual property (IP). Ever careful about limiting consumption rate, new businesses might be enticed to concede interest in licensed property assurance. To the people who have made an effort not to safeguard intellectual property, it feels complicated and costly. Time and again, new companies wind up relinquishing licensed property freedoms by failing to safeguard their thoughts and developments.

A few basic and financially savvy procedures can limit the uneasiness, yet assist with safeguarding center resources.

Organizations once in a while feel that patent security is the best way to safeguard themselves. New companies regularly overlook the worth of non-patent licensed property. While licenses can be staggeringly important, it doesn't be guaranteed that an organization's item is a decent item or that it will sell well. Proprietary advantages, network safety strategies, brand names, and copyrights can all be types of IP that can be safeguarded.

Here is a synopsis of the kinds of licensed property insurances accessible:

Licenses

Licenses are the best security you can get for another item. A patent gives its creator the option to keep others from making, utilizing, or selling the protected topic depicted in the patent's cases. The main points of contention in deciding if you can get a patent are: Just the substantial exemplification of a thought, equation, or item is patentable; the development should be new or novel; the creation should not have been protected or portrayed in a printed distribution beforehand, and ultimately the innovation should have some valuable reason. In the US you get a patent from the U.S. Patent and Trademark Office, however, this cycle can require quite a while and be confounded. You normally need a patent legal counselor to draw up the patent application for you. The disadvantage of licenses is that they can be costly to acquire and require quite a while.

Copyrights

Copyrights cover unique works of creation, like workmanship, promoting duplicate, books, articles, music, motion pictures, programming, and so on. A copyright gives the proprietor the select right to make duplicates of the work and to plan subordinate works (like spin-offs or corrections) in view of the work.

Brand names

A brand name right safeguards the representative worth of a word, name, image, or gadget that the brand name proprietor utilizations to recognize or recognize its products from those of others. A few notable brand names incorporate the Coca-Cola brand name, American Express brand name, and IBM brand name. You get the freedom to a brand name by really involving the imprint in business. You don't have to enroll in the imprint to get privileges to it, however, government enlistment offers a few benefits. You register an imprint with the U.S. Patent and Trademark Office.

Safeguard Your Own Resources by Shaping the Business as a Company or LLC

Never start a business as a "sole ownership," which can bring about your own resources being in danger for the obligations and liabilities of the business. You will quite often need to begin the business as an S enterprise (giving you good move-through charge treatment), a C partnership (which most funding financial backers hope to see), or a Limited Liability Company (LLC). None of those are especially costly or challenging to set up. My own inclination is to begin the business as an S enterprise, which can then effectively be changed over completely to a C organization as you get financial backers and issue numerous classes of stock.

Numerous entrepreneurs, nonetheless, are under the mixed-up impression that they are totally safeguarded from individual obligation by documenting a Testament of Joining for a partnership. This isn't accurate. The simple course of consolidating doesn't totally safeguard the entrepreneurs. To reduce the probability of such private or investor obligation, you ought to try to stick to specific systems:

Continuously utilize the corporate name. The name of the partnership ought to be utilized in full, including "Inc." or "Corp." on all agreements, solicitations, or records utilized by the company. This obviously shows the presence of the partnership as a different element.

Continuously utilize legitimate marks. This implies that you will sign for the partnership, utilizing the name of the organization and your title. You ought to regularly utilize the following configuration while marking contracts in the interest of the organization:

Partnership NAME

By: _____

Your name - approved marking an official and corporate title

Follow every single corporate convention. This incorporates following local laws, giving stock appropriately, holding gatherings of the Directorate, recording the gathering minutes, and following other corporate customs.

Try to keep supports discrete

Corporate assets and the assets of individual investors ought not to be in similar records or joined under any condition.

Make a point to keep tax collection discrete

The organization's duties ought to be paid completely from corporate records and separate government forms petitioned for the partnership.

All exchanges made by the enterprise ought to be plainly isolated from any singular exchanges

Basically, by never obscuring the line between individual investors, proprietors, or the Directorate, and the organization (which remains as a different substance), you run less risk on any private liabilities for the obligations of the business.

Think of an Extraordinary Name for Your Business

Choosing the right name for your startup can altogether affect your business achievement. Some unacceptable names could result in difficult legitimate and business obstacles. Here are a few fundamental tips on the most proficient method to name your startup:

Keep away from hard-to-spell names

Try not to pick a name that could be restricted as your business develops.
Lead an intensive Web search on a proposed name.
Get a ".com" space name (instead of ".net" or another variation).

Direct an intensive brand name search

Ensure you and your representatives will be cheerful saying the name.
Concoct five names you like and test market the name with imminent workers, partners, financial backers, and expected clients.

Center around Building an Incredible Item — However, Don't Consume A huge chunk of time to Send off

While beginning, your item or administration must be to some degree great on the off chance that not incredible. It should be separated in some significant manner from the contributions of your competition. All the other things follow this key rule. Try not to dawdle on getting your item on a mission to showcase, since early client input is one of the most outstanding ways of working on your item. Obviously, you need a "minimum viable product" (MVP) in any case, however, even that item ought to be great and separated from the opposition. Having a better test item works for some new businesses as they resolve the bugs from client responses.

Fabricate an Incredible Site for Your Organization

You ought to commit time and work to build an extraordinary site for your business. Planned financial backers, clients, and partners will look at your site, and you need to dazzle them with an expert item.

Researching The Dream And Lease

A business thought remains so until it is executed. What is it that you believe should do and accomplish? Figure out all that you might need about anything business at any point. Comprehend the business and what works and what doesn't. For a business to be a triumph it should satisfy a need and/or offer something individuals need. Tips on interesting points are:

Is your business thought remarkable?

Who will be your clients and what are their necessities?

Where and who are your producers/providers?

What gear do you want?

How might you get the item or administration to the client?

Do you want business premises, licenses, or grants?

Is it safe to say that you are recruiting workers?

What is a sensible cost to pay for your item or administration?

Will that cost cover expenses and make the business suitable?

Gathering information is urgent to assist you with arranging the fate of your organization. Investigating the monetary information of comparable organizations will assist you with finding out about expenses and potential income.

Gathering information will likewise assist you with grasping expected clients' requirements so you can focus on a particular client base and decide how best to reach and administer those clients. Great client support which produces positive verbal proposals is a definitive method for promoting your business and assisting it with development.

A savvy strategy is critical while laying out another business. Strategies are a rule to keep to take the business from the fire up to extension. A marketable strategy can give direction and clearness as to business objectives and how you intend to accomplish them and thusly make it simpler to source funds from monetary establishments and likely financial backers. A serviceable strategy likewise assists you with supporting your efficiency by keeping you focussed on the ideal results.

Your field-tested strategy ought to respond to any inquiries concerning the execution of your business thought, eg. how you will manage contenders and different dangers, proposed administration systems, and your deals targets opposite your monetary responsibilities to decide the expected effect on your capital.

Decide Business Construction and Limit Chance

A fruitful business visionary isolates their own life from the business. However, another business is a basic piece of an entrepreneur's life, in a perfect world pick a business structure that assists with keeping business capital and income separate from your budgets on the off chance that things don't work out as expected.

Different business structures convey various dangers and entrepreneurs might be by and by at risk for whatever turns out badly. Ensure you know about any authoritative and permitting prerequisites and guarantee you go along before you send off your business. Employ experts to direct you and ensure you have the right situation and records set up to oversee and control your business, for example, bookkeeping programming and provider contracts. Consider work environment, well-being and security prerequisites and play it safe to limit risk where conceivable.

Area and Workers

If you want business premises, contemplate reasonable areas and consider protection, and the continuous expenses of leasing a business property and the agreements of the rent understanding which might be burdensome. You may likewise have to enlist workers. Consider your business structure, the business you are in and the work the representative will do concerning your area, and your commitments to your workers, as these can vary per state or region.

If you intend to rent office space for Your Business, Spotlight these major questions

Renting office space is quite possibly the biggest cost a startup can cause. Arranging the most ideal rent can set aside your organization enough money to enlist a couple of additional workers or send off another showcasing effort.

Remember that your capacity to arrange an office rent is reliant upon the amount of influence you possess. Get your work done. Are different organizations competing for a similar space? Has the space been empty for quite a while? Factors, for example, may mean the distinction between you making major decisions, or a landowner demanding grave terms all through the rent cycle.

Since no rent is standard, here are a few ideas to assist you with turning into somewhat more rent clever and arranging a positive office rent for your startup:

Length of the rent term

Property managers are commonly ready to make concessions for longer-term leases. Nonetheless, your organization's requirements might change and you could wind up getting into rent for an office space that is excessively little, too large, or with a lease that is above-market assuming interest for space thusly declines. Attempt to arrange a more limited term rent with recharging choices: a two-year rent with a two-year reestablishment choice, for example, instead of a four-year rent.

Occupant upgrades

Your new space might require a few upgrades or modifications (another paintwork, new covering, a reconfiguration of the space). Which party will pay for these upgrades relies heavily on how tight the business office space market is in your city. Most structure leases specify that the occupant can't make any changes or upgrades without the landowner's assent. Request a statement that says you can make changes or upgrades with the property manager's assent, and that the assent will not be irrationally kept, deferred, or molded. Frequently, you can arrange an "occupant improvement stipend," which is settled upon the amount of cash that the property manager will accommodate the upgrades and modifications you might want to make.

Endlessly lease accelerations

A few property managers will give complimentary housing to the principal for a little while of rent. Fixed lease over longer-term leases is generally uncommon. At times property managers demand yearly increments in light of the rate expansions in the Consumer Price Index (CPI). Assuming your landowner demands lease accelerations, attempt to set up a CPI lease increment that doesn't kick in for basically the initial two years of the term. Then, at that point, attempt to get a cap on how much every year's increment. On the off chance that you need to live with a lease heightening proviso, attempt to arrange a foreordained fixed increment.

Fixes, upgrades, and substitutions

Know about a proviso that expresses that toward the finish of the rent you should re-establish the premises to their unique condition. Attempt to arrange a provision that expresses the following: "The premises will be gotten back to the Landowner toward the finish of the tenure in a similar condition as toward the start of the occupancy, barring (1) common mileage, (2) harm by fire and undeniable loss not the shortcoming of the inhabitant, and (3) changes recently supported by the Property manager."

Task and renting

New businesses ought to haggle sufficient adaptability in the task and renting conditions to consider consolidations, redesigns, and share proprietorship changes. Keep an eye out for a provision that says an adjustment of over half of the organization's stock proprietorship will be considered a task that is restricted without the landowner's earlier endorsement. As your organization develops and new individuals put resources into it, this provision can be accidentally set off.

Attempt to stay away from uneven rent arrangements

Landowners use structure rent arrangements that can be exceptionally uneven. Be keeping watch and haggle on these sorts of arrangements that are intensely property manager ideal:

The landowner is given the option to give to the occupant, unbounded, expanded working expenses, for example, local charges, building fixes, or insurance payments.
The property manager attempts to rent the premises "with no guarantees" or attempts to disavow liability regarding consistency with natural regulations or the Americans with Disabilities Act (ADA).
The landowner attempts to require the occupant to pay any expense increments coming about because of an offer of the property.
The landowner attempts to claim all authority to end the rent at the property manager's comfort.
The property manager attempts to restrict the chance of renting or task.
The landowner demands individual assurance from the critical investors of the organization.

Trust

The main explanation clients don't buy your products isn't cost - - it's trust.

Step-by-step instructions to acquire clients' trust

First impression

Think about this: 60-80 percent of internet business webpage guests are first-time guests. The typical transformation rate for these guests - - simply 2.5 percent. All that's needed is 2.6 seconds for guests to size up your image. Furthermore, whenever you've lost those guests, the possibilities of getting them back are negligible. So what do clients see when they first land on your site?

With regards to initial feelings, there are three principal factors: a proficient plan, great UX, and a fast stacking site. Brands can further develop client trust in their site by further developing a plan, and UX, and enhancing their site speed, portable similarity, and space expert in Google. To the extent that plan, this implies utilizing pictures, textual styles, and design that looks proficient as well as focusing on variety plan and association. Exhibiting information on great UX and making client route and checkout simple and natural additionally assembles trust in your image.

At the point when guests initially get to a site, they retain the plan. From that point onward, a UX Matters heat map concentrates on showing how their eyes move towards parts of the page where trust signals are found.

Flaunting inclusion in notable distributions, trust checks, and publicizing recognizable installment techniques cause the client to feel great.

Social confirmation

This is the main stage in trust evaluation. A lot of destinations can have an extraordinary plan and establish heavenly first connections - yet would they say they are ready to push clients to the subsequent stage in evaluation?

In this stage, research shows that proposals are the main trust factor, and 92 percent of individuals trust suggestions from individuals they know, and 70 percent trust customer assessments posted on the web. So this is where surveys come in. Customers are searching for genuine client suppositions on outsider locales to see what different customers need to say.

They're likewise inspecting client-created photographs and recordings to check whether the item matches what is publicized. Individuals are turning out to be significantly less dependable on brand promotion, and substantially more trusting of other customer assessments.

Risk evaluation

After a client has begun to accept a site is reliable, they start the risk evaluation process. In this stage, the major questions of trust are the manner by which secure their own data is and the way that dependable it is for them to make a buy.

One more method for building trust during this stage is to offer exhaustive, simple-to-track-down contact data. The last thing a client needs is to give up their delicate data and cash and never see their item. Diminish the risk of buying by including different choices to reach you, such as a live visit, telephone number (ideally complimentary), and email address. Likewise, incorporate FAQs, merchandise exchanges, and bundle following in a profoundly noticeable region.

Spread the word about certain you show that you acknowledge well installment strategies and keeping in mind that they're in the checkout stages, keep on flaunting site tributes that underscore your client assistance to urge them to trust you enough to buy.

From client to rehash customer

After you've worked a client's trust and they've bought from you, the excursion isn't finished. In this stage, you need to transform that client into a brand advocate who can assist you with procuring new customers.

The way into this is obviously giving an amazing first purchasing experience. Ensure you give administration clients will need to go wild about and that will bring them back.

Urge past customers to leave audits and submit photographs of them with their items, so you can re-use these in advertising to draw in new customers. You can likewise offer coupons as an additional impetus for them to then share these surveys and photographs on friendly. Offering a coupon likewise takes them back to your store - - expanding the opportunity that they will buy from you in the future.

Acquiring client trust online is difficult, yet assuming you focus on how trust structures all through different touch focus in the customer venture, you can urge more clients to purchase and keep on getting back to your web-based business store.

Development

Development and imagination are frequently utilized equivalently. While comparative, they're not something very similar. Involving imagination in business is significant because it cultivates remarkable thoughts. This oddity is a vital part of development.

For a plan to be creative, it should likewise be helpful. Inventive thoughts don't necessarily prompt advancements since they won't be guaranteed to deliver reasonable answers for issues.

Development is an item, administration, plan of action, or procedure that is both novel and valuable. Developments don't need to be significant in innovation or new plans of action; they can be pretty much as straightforward as moves up to an organization's client support or elements added to a current item.

Significance of development

It encourages development

Stagnation can be very unfavorable to your business. Accomplishing hierarchical and monetary development through advancement is vital to remain above water in the present profoundly cutthroat world.

It isolates organizations from their opposition

Most ventures are populated with different contenders offering comparable items or administrations. Advancement can recognize your business from others.

Testing Your Business Ideas

Testing your business idea is critical to check whether it is a suitable plan of action.
Try not to race into sending off an item; without cautious thought and arranging, it very well may be a misuse of basic assets on the off chance that it comes up short.

Do you have a thought for the following huge thing? You might think your thought is wonderful how it is, yet it's wise to test it before you invest energy and cash fostering a business or item for which there's no market. The following are eight moves toward assisting you with ensuring your item thought is something the world needs before you send off it.

Testing a business's thoughts is urgent to its prosperity. On the off chance that you aimlessly expect a thought will be a success, you're risking a lot of time, cash, and different assets to put resources into its send-off. Organizations frequently skirt this step since they're eager to send off their item. They don't make a field-tested strategy or plan of action in view of their market testing/research, chasing after their business process without a guide. Also, they neglect to distinguish precisely who their ideal interest group is. Until you test your thought, you won't realize who will think that it is valuable. Without this data, your showcasing could fail to be noticed, wasting your time with your item thought: regardless of whether it's an extraordinary one.

The following are moves toward testing your business thought to decide its incentive.

Construct a base practical item

Following the lean startup, a model is an incredible method for fostering your business or a particular item. In particular, you need to fabricate a minimum viable product (MVP).

An MVP is the easiest type of your thought that you can really sell as an item. Utilizing the standards of rendition of the item to test and market right off the bat in the improvement cycle so that any changes or changes are in light of genuine criticism from the interest group.

Show it to a gathering of pundits

At the point when you have your most memorable model or test administration prepared, present it to potential objective clients.

You ought to converse with a few possible clients, to check whether they relate to the issue the same way you do. At the end of the day, you really want to see whether this is a genuine issue for a larger part of your objective market or only a couple.

Be that as it may, to painstakingly really scrutinize your new business thought, select your likely clients.

Distinguish individuals in that target you know to be distrustful and basic. These individuals could be furious clients from past experiences or companions who generally take the glass-half-void point of view.

Make a promotion plan and use it

All of the preliminary work amounts to nothing on the off chance that you don't perform an adequate number of activities to get a decent proportion of reaction. When you have a feasible item, you want to follow up on the premium in it.

If you do this, you will have information on your item. You'll realize who is keen on it, what advertising methodologies worked and didn't work, and how you can improve, which are all significant stages in getting your thought and business going.

Embrace a trial and error mentality

An excessive number of organizations are reluctant to come up short, so they don't set themselves in that frame of mind to do as such. Frequently, this looks like either evasion of seeking after novel thoughts or inability to test an item thought before sending off it appropriately.

By embracing a trial and error mentality, you'll be more able to commit errors and test a wide range of thoughts. Your plan of action will open all the more long-haul esteem, as you'll allow more thoughts on an opportunity to work out as expected. In this situation, disappointment is likewise viewed as a triumph, as it permits you to more readily comprehend what works and what doesn't in this ever-changing business world.

Execute configuration thinking

Configuration thinking includes the mental, vital and reasonable cycles of growing groundbreaking thoughts or items. It assists pioneers with rethinking issues and making better, more effective fixes. As such, it makes the way for additional pivotal disclosures and innovations.

To carry out this system in your business, you need to follow the five phases of configuration thinking: compassion (research/grasp clients' requirements), characterize (express your clients' concerns and needs), ideate (conceptualize special answers for their concerns), model (make the arrangements) and, in particular, test (give them a shot yourself).

www.ingramcontent.com/pod-product-compliance
Lightning Source LLC
Chambersburg PA
CBHW070318220526
45465CB00004B/1893